BABYSITTING 101

THE OFFICIAL BABYSITTING HANDBOOK

REBECCA S. COLMER

W9-BFN-866

Babysitting 101
By Rebecca S. Colmer

Published by: Eklektika Press
               Post Office Box 157
               Chelsea, MI 48118

This book may not be reproduced in whole or in part in any form by any means. Written permission must be secured from the publisher to use or reproduce any part of this book.

Copyright © 1996 by Rebecca S. Colmer
Printed in the United States of America

Library of Congress Catalog Card Number: 96-96476
Colmer, Rebecca S.
Babysitting 101: The Official Babysitting Handbook

ISBN   0-965 1672-1-6   : $9.95   Softcover

Warning-Disclaimer

The information in this book is not intended to serve as a
replacement for medical care, nor to replace the services of a
trained health professional. This book is not a comprehensive
overview of babysitting. If medical assistance is needed consult a
physician or a health care professional before following
any of the proposed courses of treatment.

CONTENTS

GENERAL BABYSITTING TIPS

CHOW, BATH, AND BEDTIME

ENTERTAINMENT

HOUSEHOLD EMERGENCIES

BASIC FIRST AID

MEDICAL EMERGENCIES

ACKNOWLEDGMENT

Thanks to all of the babysitters and parents who
contributed to this handbook.

Special thanks to Dr. Amy Ochs and Dr. Malcolm
Colmer for their careful evaluation of the medical
emergency and first-aid tips.

Thanks to Tony & Shelly Gray for their
motivation and support.

Thanks to Flip.

Cover and book design by Joe DiPalma.

1
How to be the Best Babysitter

"BE PREPARED" should be the official babysitter's motto. Babysitting is a big responsibility and you should be as prepared as possible. Prior to your first babysitting job, consider the following:

Take a babysitting course. Contact your school, the local "Y", hospital or local community center to get enrolled. Read. Go to the library and read books on child care and child rearing. Volunteer to help at your church nursery or a local day care facility. Take a cardiopulmonary resuscitation (CPR) and/or first aid course. Speak with friends who currently babysit, and ask them to share their experiences.

2
Check with your parents before you start!

Check with your parents before you start babysitting.
Will babysitting take away too much time from school or family activities?
Do you really have enough spare time to babysit?
Do you have younger brothers and sisters to take care of?
Would your parents object to weeknight babysitting?
Would your parents object to you staying out past midnight on weekends?
Talk things over with your parents and make sure everyone is in agreement.

3
How to get the job!

Get the word out.
Ask fellow babysitters to recommend you when they are unable to take the job.
Print a flier or brochure and pass it out to your friends and neighbors.
Post a flier on your house of worship's bulletin board.
Ask your parents to tell their friends and associates about you.
Run an inexpensive ad in your local newspaper. Let them know you have read "Babysitting 101."

4

What to ask during the client interview!

Ask how many children you will be
caring for and their ages.
Ask the date and length of time you
will be needed to babysit.
Negotiate your rate of pay. Some babysitters
charge a flat rate for one child and an additional
$1.00 per child. Some babysitters charge time
and a half for any time after midnight
Arrange reliable (sober) transportation
to and from your job.
Write down the full name, address, and
telephone number of your client.
Different geographical regions pay different
hourly rates; ask around and find out what the
"going rate" is. Be flexible while
you are building your experience.
Ask if the children have any special needs.

5
What to take on the job!

This book: Babysitting 101
Client Information Sheet
Basic first aid kit
Pad and pencil or pen
Change/money
Flashlight
Game bag that may include:
-crayons/markers
-coloring books
-paper dolls
-toy trucks
-1 or 2 videos
-puppets
-legos
-books
-cards
-T-shirt painting kit
-friendship bracelet kit

6

How and when to get paid!

The terms of your employment should
be agreed upon before you arrive
on the job. Know how long you
will be expected to
work, and how much you will
be paid. Request to be paid
in full before you go home.
If the parents do not have cash, and
do not wish to write you a check, you
should prepare a quick bill for them.
The bill should include the date and
number of hours worked, and the amount
owed. Tell them that you will call them
tomorrow or whenever it's most
convenient to make arrangements
for getting paid.

7

What if you get sick and have to cancel?

A good babysitter should not cancel unless he or she is sick, or if there is a family emergency. You should give your client as much notice as possible.

Provide your client with a name of alternate babysitters that you would recommend.

Have the list of names and telephone numbers available should they ask.

8

What to wear on the job?

You should be clean, well groomed,
and wear loose, comfortable clothing.
Wear washable clothes. The parents
will not expect you to get
dressed up. Blue jeans are fine.
You should wear sneakers or
flat shoes.

If you are babysitting for
a young baby, keep in mind they
like to grab at shimmering items
like dangling earrings
and necklaces.

9

How old should you be when you start babysitting?

Most babysitters are between the ages of eleven and thirteen when they start babysitting. If you are not old enough to babysit on your own, you might consider starting out as a babysitter's assistant for one of your friends. Make sure to check with the client, in advance. When you first start babysitting, start out slowly. Your first few jobs might be afternoon jobs. Age is not the most important factor. Attitude, responsiblity, and a mature approach to your job are equally important.

10
Is babysitting just for girls?

NO! There are many boys who enjoy babysitting. It is no longer just a girl's job to take care of the children.

Some little boys actually prefer having a male babysitter. They like having a male role model to look up to.

11

Do you like children?

If children get under your skin most of the time, then babysitting is probably not the job for you.

Do you like children of all ages? If handling small babies makes you nervous, you should probably pass up those jobs.

Be honest about what you do and do not like.

12
Babysitting Clubs

There are hundreds of babysitting
clubs throughout the United States.
If there is not a babysitting club
in your area, start your own.
Check the yellow pages.

By sharing ideas you will
become a better babysitter.

13

What to do if you get sick on the job!

If you get sick on the job, call your parents and ask them to help you.

DO NOT LEAVE THE CHILD ALONE.

If you cannot reach your parents, call a friend or another babysitter to assist you.

14

What to do if your client doesn't call you back after the first job

Call the client to explain your concerns.

Let the client know you enjoyed babysitting for their child.

Ask for some feedback.

Let him (or her) know that you are available for more babysitting jobs.

15
How many children can you manage easily?

More than three children is probably too many children for one person to babysit. If there are more than three children get an additional babysitter.

If, during the initial interview with the client, you find out there is more than one child, it could be useful to get the telephone number of the past babysitter, to get a background on the dispositions of the children.

Remember, you are responsible for the children under your care. Do not take on more than you can handle.

16
Does babysitting include housekeeping?

General tidying-up is part of the babysitter's responsibility. However, major cleaning should be an additional fee. It is important to straighten up the house before the parents get home.

If your client asks you to do extra cleaning while you are there, be straightforward and ask for additional pay. It may feel a little awkward, but your client may not realize he or she is taking advantage of you.

17

Is it okay to have company while babysitting?

You should not have any visitors while you are babysitting, without prior permission from your client.
If any of your friends show up while you are babysitting, remind them you are working and will have to visit with them at another time.

18
Babysitting for children of divorced parents

Stay neutral. Do not take sides.
Do not push the child to talk about his
feelings. Respect his privacy.
Make arrangements in advance to get
a ride home since a single parent will
not be able to leave the child alone in
order to take you home.

19
Babysitting for a disabled child

If the child you are babysitting is
disabled, either mentally or physically,
he/she may need extra care.
Get special instructions from the parents
before they leave.

20
Family Pets

Ask the parents if there are any
special instructions for taking care
of the family pet.
Does the dog have to be walked?
Does the cat have to be fed?
Ask if pets are to be kept inside or outside,
or both. In case of an emergency,
it is always best to have the veterinarian's
telephone number close at hand.

21
Telephone Tips

Ask the parents for instructions for
answering the telephone.
Some parents may prefer to let the
answering machine pick up.
If you answer the phone, do not give
out unnecessary information.
Hang up on obscene phone calls.

22

Things to do before the parents leave

Arrive 10-15 minutes early so that the child can start to adjust to you.

Have parents complete the Client Information and Consent & Payment Forms.

Review completed Client Information with the client.

Take a house tour (refer to tip #23).

23
What should the house tour include?

Before the parents leave make sure you get a tour of the house. You should be able to locate and/or operate the following:

- Lights- inside and outside
- Thermostat
- Television
- VCR
- Telephone/answering machine
- Microwave
- Stove and Oven
- Alarm System
- Flashlight
- First Aid Kit

24
Know where you are!

Write down the exact address and telephone number of where you are babysitting. Make sure that you know the parents' full names.
Sometimes during an emergency it is easy to become confused and not remember the details of where you are babysitting.
Write it down on the list of 10 important numbers.

25
Ten important phone numbers to always have on hand

·911
·Police
·Fire
·Poison Control Center
·Ambulance
·Pediatrician/doctor
·Telephone number(s) where parents can be reached at all times
·Neighbors (2)
·Additional Babysitters
·Clients' home and office telephone numbers

26
Other important telephone numbers

·Electric Company
·Gas Company
·Taxi
·Dentist
·Animal Control
·Veterinarian
·Your parents' telephone number

27

What if the parents get home late?

If the parents are late returning home, call your parents and keep them advised of the situation.
Try to stay awake. Always stay within hearing range of the children.

When the parents arrive, let them know that you were worried. Suggest they call and let you know the next time they are running late.

28

What if the parents appear intoxicated when they return?

If the parents appear intoxicated,
do not get in the car with them.
Call your parents.
When they answer, casually say,
"The Smiths just got home. You can
come and get me now. Thanks."

(Rehearse this rescue dialog, in advance,
with your parents.)

29

What if a parent makes a pass at you?

If a parent makes suggestive remarks or tries to touch you in an inappropriate manner, you do not have to go along with it.

You deserve to be treated with respect. Simply say, "Please do not do that, it makes me uncomfortable."

Don't babysit for that family again. Tell your parents.

30

What if you suspect child abuse?

Accusations of child abuse have very serious consequences. Be very cautious before you make such a statement.

First, tell your parents what you suspect and why. They will probably have good advice on what to do next.

Do not gossip about your suspicions. If your suspicions are correct, the family will need lots of help. If your suspicions are incorrect, you could cause irreparable damage to the family's reputation and to your own.

31

How to handle separation anxiety

If the child begins to cry while the
parents are leaving, don't worry. Usually
the tears do not last very long.
Remain calm and cheerful.
Try the following:
Wave good-bye.
Start an activity-video, board game,
or read a book.
Distract the child with his favorite toy.
Ask for the child's help in getting a
glass of water or finding the bathroom, etc.
Sing a song.
Remind the child the parents are
going to return.

32
Dependence Vs. Independence

Sometimes the child will get confused
about whether he wants to be dependent
or independent. He may not be sure if he
wants to be helped or left on his own.
Whenever possible, let him do or try to
do as much for himself as he wants.
Stand by patiently without offering
help or advice, unless he asks you.
Encourage him.
Congratulate him on his successes.

33
Discipline

Ask the parents how they discipline their child. Make sure that good behavior gets rewarded and bad behavior does not.

Be positive. "Do" works much better than "Do Not."

Sometimes it is necessary to take a "time out." The child is sent to another room for a few minutes. Set a timer. Determine the time limit by their age. For example, three-year-olds should take a three minute time out. Explain to them that they need to calm down.

When the timer goes off, welcome the child back. Let them know that you didn't like their behavior, but you still like the child.

A babysitter should never strike or spank a child.

34
Sibling Squabbles

If siblings get into a squabble, try
to let them work it out themselves.
Suggest a compromise.
Ask them to play separately until
they think they can get along.

35

How to get a child to listen to you

Respect the child's rights.
Listen to his opinions. Let him know that his
opinions are important.
Offer the child choices.

36
Be a good role model

Children notice what you do and the
way you do it. Always try to set
a good example.

Do not be rude.

Always say
please and thank you.

Show the children courtesy
and respect.

Clean up after yourself.

Never smoke or drink
alcoholic beverages.

37
Courtesy

If the parent tells you to help yourself to a snack,
do not pig out and eat everything in sight.
Do not make long distance calls.
Do not snoop around.
Treat the house you are in as if you are a guest.

38

Respect the family values

When you babysit, you have to respect other people's values, even if you do not agree. Do not try to change or criticize their ways of raising their children.

Be respectful of their religious practices. Do not impose your own beliefs on other people's children.

39
Babysitting in your own home

Make sure that your home is child-proofed.
Be aware of stairs that small children like to
climb. You may want to put a gate at the entrance
to prevent playing on the stairs.
Install electrical outlet guards if possible.
Do not let the child get into cupboards where
household cleaners are stored.
Know where the potential hazards are and keep
children away from those areas.
Make sure all medicines including aspirin and
Tylenol are out of reach.

40
Overnight babysitting

Staying overnight is a tremendous
responsibility. Make sure that you are
qualified, and prepared.
Ask the parents to call frequently.
More than likely, the parent will pay you
a flat fee rather than an hourly rate.

41
Taking children outside to play

Get permission from the parents to take
the child outside to play.
Do not let the child get too much sun.
Apply a sunscreen.
Always keep the child in your sight.
Never turn away from the child,
even for a moment.
Be especially careful crossing streets.
Obey all traffic signals.

42
Chow Time

Check to make sure the child has no allergies. The parents should leave instructions on what to feed the child for lunch and dinner.

It is a good idea to feed children at the kitchen or dining room table. This avoids the chance of spilling food or drink on the furniture or carpet.

A child younger than two years should not be given honey. A baby cannot digest the spores it may contain, and that could cause food poisoning. A pre-two year old should never be given raisins, nuts, melon, corn, cherries, berries, or chocolate, for they are too hard on the digestive system, and some of them can choke a young child.

43
Feeding the baby

Feed the baby when he is hungry and burp him when he is full. Check with parents for formula preparation instructions. They should also tell you how often the baby likes to be fed. Ask the parents how much the bottle needs to be heated, and how you should prepare it. Always test the temperature of the formula before giving it to the baby.

Never give the baby a bottle that has been sitting around the house. The milk could be curdled.

Hold the baby at a slight angle to elevate the head while feeding. Hold the baby in one arm while feeding with the other.

If the baby cries while you are trying to feed him, check for a clogged nipple. If the baby is not hungry, do not force him to take the bottle. Try a different position.

Be patient while trying to burp the baby. Hold him against your shoulder and pat firmly on the back.

44

Snacks for babies with only a few teeth

Most babies with only a few teeth like to snack on:
Vanilla Wafers
Cheerios
Graham Crackers
Saltines

Check with the parents to find out what their baby may eat for a snack.
Pay close attention to the child to make sure he isn't choking.
Children under age 2 shouldn't have peanuts or popcorn. If given hotdogs, they should be cut into tiny pieces.

45
Kitchen safety

The kitchen contains all sorts of possible dangers. The kitchen is clearly not the place to be careless.
Never leave a child alone in the kitchen.
Aim all pot handles to the back of the stove so that the child cannot knock over pots.
Keep cabinet doors closed.
Don't store tempting foods near the stove.
Make sure that plastic bags are out of reach of children.
Push small appliances to the back of countertops.
Use unbreakable plates and mugs for children.

46

Easy to prepare simple meals

Peanut Butter and Jelly Sandwiches
Soup and Sandwiches
Hotdogs
Macaroni and Cheese
Cereal
Scrambled Eggs
Grilled Cheese Sandwiches

47

How to change a diaper

It's a good idea to gather all of your supplies before you start to change the diaper. You will need the following:
· A new clean diaper
· Diaper wipes or a warm moist washcloth

· Change the baby's diaper at waist high level or on the floor.
· To prevent squirming while you change a young baby, give him a special toy for each hand
· Lay the new diaper under the baby before you slip off the soiled diaper.
· Slip off the soiled diaper.
· Wipe the baby's bottom, from front to back, with a diaper wipe or moist washcloth.
· For disposable diapers, the sticky tabs go at the back and fold around toward the front.
· For cloth diapers pin the front tabs over the back tabs.

48
Bath Time

Risks in the bathroom include slipping, scalding, electrocution, and poisoning, just to name a few. It is easy to avoid these dangers by taking some precautions.
Check with the parent about bath time rules, and rituals. Once the children are in the tub, they usually enjoy taking a bath. A few bubbles will always help.
Gather all of your supplies ahead of time- shampoo, toys, towels, pajamas.
Run the water and test it, with your elbow, before the child gets in. When you turn off the faucet, turn off the hot water first, cold water last.
NEVER LEAVE A CHILD ALONE IN THE TUB - EVEN TO ANSWER THE TELEPHONE!
Keep all appliances well away from the bathtub. Keep them unplugged.
Only use unbreakable bottles, containers, and cups in the bathtub.
Wipe up spills immediately.

49
Bedtime

Try to keep the pre-bedtime hour enjoyable.
Always make sure that the child knows the
bedtime hour is approaching.
Be familiar with the bedtime ritual.
Dim the lights and speak in low, hushed tones.
Enjoy a bedtime story together.
Most children's bedtime routines include snack,
go potty, brush teeth, sometimes a bath, story,
sometimes a prayer, and then bed.

50
How to handle a fussy crying baby at bedtime

Dim the lights as much as possible.
Gently rock the baby while listening to
soothing music.
Check to see if the baby has a soiled diaper.
Make sure that the baby is not tangled
in his blankets.
Give the baby a bottle.
Check to make sure that the baby is
not too hot.
Stay in the room with the baby for several
minutes after he has fallen asleep.

51

Once the child goes to sleep

Check on the child every half hour.
Pick up toys, books, clothes, etc. Clean up any
messes that may have been made.
Clean up the kitchen.
Keep the volume setting on the television or
stereo turned on low.
Limit the amount of time you use the phone. The
parents may be trying to call you.
Stay awake until the parents arrive home.

52

Entertaining babies...

Babies like things that rattle and jingle,
and make lots of noise.

Babies like to listen while you read aloud.

Babies like to be sung to; they like
to listen to music.

Babies like to play Peek-A-Boo.

Babies like bright colors.

Babies like to be held.

It really doesn't take much to
entertain small babies. Most importantly,
keep them safe. Check their
diaper regularly.

53
How to entertain a toddler (age 1-3)

A child this age is into everything.
Toddlers are busy and curious. They can be
exciting and exhausting.
Their moods often change rapidly.
Toddlers like to knock over blocks, and when
you are not watching, will take apart
anything else they can find.
Toddlers like to play Hide and Seek, Mother
May I?, and Duck, Duck, Goose.
They like to stack blocks, dress dolls, and play
with clay. Of course, they like to color too.

54

How to entertain 3-6 year olds

This age child sometimes like to play
with you, not just beside you. Three to
six year olds like to try simple reading,
but also enjoy listening to you read more
complicated stories.

Three to six year olds like to play
cards. Go Fish and Old Maid are
long time favorites.

They also like to play marbles and jacks.
Board games are always a lot of fun.

55

How to entertain 6-10 year olds

After children reach elementary school age, babysitting is usually much easier. It is like taking care of a younger friend.

These children like to watch videos. They like to read. Most children like to be helped with their homework.

Six to ten year olds like to paint, cook simple meals, play with their toys. (Some parents may not want their child cooking, so get permission before the parents leave.)

56

Know the favorites

Before the parents leave find out the child's favorites:

Toy
Book
Bedtime Story
Game
Song
Food
Beverage
Chair

57

Good Reading, Anytime

The Cat in the Hat by Dr. Seuss

Curious George by H.A. Ray

The Little Engine That Could by Watty Piper

Madeline by Ludwig Bemelmans

Noisy Nora by Rosemary Wells

Pretend You're a Cat by Jean Marzollo

The Story of Babar by Laurent de Brunhoff

Tom and Pippo's Day by Helen Oxenbury

The Veleveteen Rabbit by Margery Williams

Where's Waldo? by Martin Handford

58

Great Read Aloud Books

Charlotte's Wed by E.B. White

Stuart Little by E.B. White

The Thirteen Clocks by James Thurber

Eloise by Kay Thompson

Charlie and the Great Glass Elevator
by Ronald Dahl

Land of Oz (series) by Frank Baum

59

Teaching Books

A to Zoo by Carolyn W. Lima

Is your Mama a Llama by Deborah Guarino

Toolbox by Anne Rockwell

William the Vehicle King by Laura Newton

The Magic Schoolbus (series) by Joanna Cole

Anno's Counting Book by Mitsumasa Anno

60
Fun games to play

- Play cooking. Collect small plastic containers and lids. Arrange on a tray, serve your guests.

- Tea Party

- Post Office. Arrange stationary and envelopes. Deliver the mail.

- Finger Painting.

- Make things out of clay or homemade play dough.

- Playacting

- Card Games

- Board Games

- Activity Kits

61

Crafts to make

- Fold paper hats out of newspaper. Color them and decorate.

- Make masks out of paper bags.

- Make aluminum foil dolls.

- Collect flowers and press them into a book.

- Learn to crochet

62
Short feature videos

The Adventures of Curious George

The Cat in the Hat and Dr. Seuss on the Loose

Koko's Kitten

Tales of Beatrix Potter

The Ugly Duckling

Winnie the Pooh and the Blustery Day

Pinocchio

The Story of Babar and the Little Elephant

The Emperor and the Nightingale

63
Favorite Songs

- Ring Around the Rosie

- This Old Man

- Itsy Bitsy Spider

- Old MacDonald

- The Hokey Pokey

64
Must See Musicals

Annie

Babes in Toyland

Chitty Chitty Bang Bang

Fiddler on the Roof

Mary Poppins

The Music Man

My Fair Lady

Snow White and the Seven Dwarfs

The Sound of Music

South Pacific

65

What if there is a fire?

1. Get the child out of the house immediately.

2. Do not try to put out the fire.

3. Once you are out of the house do not go back inside to try to save favorite toys or important papers.

4. Go to the neighbor's house and call 911 or the fire department.

5. Call the parents.

66

Common Sources of Fires within the home

1. Cigarettes and matches

2. Cooking equipment

3. Kitchen grease
(do not pour water on a grease fire)

4. Home heating equipment

5. Flammable items used or stored incorrectly

6. Electrical short circuits

Ask the parents if they have smoke
detectors in their home. Find out
when they
were last checked.
Ask about fire extinguishers.

67

Fire Drills

Few things are more terrifying than a fire. Being able to act quickly and make correct decisions during a real fire could save your life.

Start your emergency planning by looking in each room and plotting out at least two ways to escape.

Make sure that any locks or latches on windows and doors, open easily from the inside.

Since smoke rises during a fire, practice crawling close to the floor where the air will be better.

Practice your home escape plan.

68
Stop, Drop, Roll

If your clothes catch on fire, you should:

Stop: Stop where you are.

Drop: Drop to the the ground and cover your face with your hands.

Roll: Roll over and over to smother the flames.

Cool: Cool the burn with water.

Call the parents.

69

If the neighbors house is on fire

If the neighbor's house is on fire, you and the child (children) should leave your home and go to a safer place in case the fire should spread.

Call your clients and let them know what you are going to do.

Be a good neighbor and call 911 to report the fire.

70
Thunder and lightning storms

- A severe thunderstorm can cause a tornado or flash flood and often knocks out electrical power.
- Lightning is always dangerous. It can start fires and cause electrical injury.
- Be alert for signs that the weather is worsening.
- If you are outside, go indoors.
- Stay away from windows and fireplaces.
- Unplug computers and appliances.
- Stay away from water. Do not take a bath or wash the dishes.
- Do not talk on the telephone.
- Stay calm and reassure your charge.
- If there is a tornado warning, go downstairs. If unsure, call your parents.

71

What to do if there is a power outage

If the power is out only in one room, or one part of the house, it is probably a blown fuse. Do not try to replace it. Let the parents take care of it when they return home.

If the power is out all over the house, it is probably a power outage. Find a flashlight or candles and matches.

Always be very careful with a lighted candle. Keep the extra matches in your pocket. Never leave a child alone with a candle.
Call the parents.
Stay calm and reassure the child.

72
What if you get locked out

Before the parents leave, it is a good idea to get a spare key from them, and keep it in your pocket.

Take the key with you if you step outside, even if for just a minute.

If, however, you do get locked out, stay calm. Go next door and ask the neighbor if you can use their phone to call your client.

73
What should you do if...

· If the phone rings? Ask the parents for specific telephone answering instructions. Some parents may prefer to let the answering machine pick up.

· If the doorbell rings? Are you or the parents expecting a visitor? If not, do not open the door. Just call out and say that the parents are not available to come to the door at this time. Ask them to leave their name and a short message.

· If a delivery person is knocking on the door. Ask him to leave the package outside the door. Leave the package there until the parents arrive.

· If there is a prowler outside? Stay calm. Call the police and tell them you are babysitting and hear sounds that are frightening. Give the police your name and address. Call a neighbor and ask them to check outside for you.

74
Basic First Aid

Minor bangs and bruises are a normal part of a child's life. It is your job to protect the child from serious hazards.

Most everyday mishaps require little or no medical attention at all. However, the child will probably like you to do something. Try soap and water. Wash the dirt out while inspecting the injury.

Band-aids may be needed to protect the cut.

Hugs and kisses always make things feel better!

75
Animal and Human Bites

If you are bitten by an animal or human, you probably need medical attention because of the chance of infection.

If a strange dog or cat bites you or the child, write down the description of the animal.

Wash the affected area with soap and water.

Put a band-aid or sterile bandage over the bite.

Get medical help.

76
Bee Stings

Bee and wasp stings are really painful. Tell the child to concentrate on taking big, deep breaths.

If the stinger is still in the wound, remove it as quickly as possible. Do not pinch the stinger because it will squirt more poison into the wound. Use tweezers to gently pull it out. To reduce pain and swelling, put something cold on the wound.

If the area swells rapidly and the child's eyes get puffy, and he has trouble breathing, this is an emergency.

Call 911 and the parents.

77
Bruises

Bruises are dark, discolored areas that may be swollen.

Apply a cold compress as soon as possible.

If the bruise is getting larger, on an arm or leg, raise it above the heart.

If it continues to enlarge, call the parents.

78
Burns and Scalds

If a burn covers an area more than the size of your hand, or is on the face or hands, it is potentially serious. Apply a cold compress and then call the parents for instructions about what to do next.

If the burned area is serious enough for medical treatment, wrap the cooled area in a clean sheet or pillow case to prevent bacteria from getting to the raw area.

First degree burn - Usually the affected area is bright red and hurts.

Second Degree burn - Any burn that blisters.

Third Degree Burn - Several layers of skin have been burned and the area usually looks white. Often there is no pain because nerves have been damaged.

Do not apply butter or any grease.

Do not break the blisters.

Call the parents.

79

Insect Bites

Most insect bites are not serious.

Wash the bite with soap and water
and apply a cold compress.

If pain, redness, swelling,
and/or red streaks
develop, call the parents.

If the parents do not respond
quickly, get medical help.

80
Nosebleeds

A nosebleed can be really scary for a child.
They look terrible, however,
rarely are they serious.

A nosebleed can be caused by a
child picking his nose, a bump on the
nose, or an object lodged in the nose.
Tell the child to remain calm and
encourage breathing through the mouth.

Have the child sit down and lean forward.
Pinch the soft part of the nose for five
minutes and place a cold compress on
the bridge of the nose.

81

Scrapes and Minor Cuts

Minor cuts need little treatment. Bleeding carries germs out of the wound and seals it as it clots.

Put the injured area under running cold water. Dry with a clean towel and cover with a band-aid or clean dressing.

Cuts on the face should be seen by a doctor if they penetrate more than the top layer of skin. Notify the parents.

Apply ice and elevate the affected area.

82
Splinters

A splinter can cause an infection.
If part of the splinter is exposed, get a
pair of tweezers and pull it out. If the child
resists and is not in pain, it can wait until the
parents get home.

If the splinter is completely under the skin, heat
a needle over a flame (to sterilize it).
Freeze the spot with an ice cube to numb
it, and gently poke the needle under
the skin to get the splinter out.

If it is a deep splinter and you cannot
get it out, call the parents. You may
need a doctor's help to remove it, and
the child may need a tetanus shot.

83
First Aid Kit

Just in case the parents do not have a
first aid kit, it is a good
idea to take your own kit.
It should include:

Band-Aids
Sterile Gauze Pads & Adhesive Tape
Neosporin or similar Antibacterial Ointment
Candle and Matches
Flashlight
Soap

Before the parents leave find out
if they have a first aid kit, and
where it is located.

84

When to call the parents

If you're uncertain about the urgency
of a medical condition, try to call
the parents first. If the situation is
urgent the parents will advise
you to call 911.

Write down the parent's instructions.

It is important to get professional help in
evaluating illness or emergency.

85
Medication

If the child you are babysitting is taking medication, make sure the parents write down specific instructions for administering the medication. It should include the exact amount to be taken and the exact time it is to be taken.

Have the parents show you what they measure and administer it in. Keep it out of reach of the children.

Never give a child medication, not even Tylenol, unless you have permission by the parents.

Never give a child aspirin on your own. In some children it could cause Reye's Syndrome.

86
Good Health Sense

Do whatever you can to keep from catching something yourself, or passing your germs on to the children.

Cover your mouth when you cough.
Wash your hands with soap and water before handling food.
Wash your hands after using the bathroom.

Be careful administering first aid.
Wash your hands before and afterward.
It is best not to touch another person's blood with your bare hands if at all possible. Use a wash cloth to clean away blood and dirt.

Keep your own immunizations up to date.

87
How to call for help

· Dial 911

· Stay calm. Take a deep breath. Speak slowly and clearly when the operator answers.
· Identify yourself: "Hello, my name is Jane Smith and I am babysitting a child..."

· State the nature of the emergency.

· State your address.

· State the telephone number from which you are calling.

· Tell the operator how many people need help.

· Listen carefully.

STAY ON THE LINE. DO NOT HANG UP UNTIL THE OPERATOR TELLS YOU TO DO SO.

88
Do No Harm

Avoid adding to the child's injuries.

Do not block an unconscious child's airway.

Never move a child who could possibly have injured his neck, back, or spine.

Do not give the child any medication, without instructions to do so.

89
Emergency vs. Basic First Aid

There are generally two types of first aid, emergency and basic. You will find some of each listed below. **THIS IS NOT A COMPLETE GUIDE TO FIRST AID.** This book does not cover artificial respiration. You should attend an artificial resuscitation training course and become certified before you start babysitting. The American Red Cross and many hospitals offer these courses.
If an emergency arises, and you are unsure of how to handle it, call 911. Call the parents.

EMERGENCY	BASIC
Unconscious Child	Bites & Stings
Breathing Difficulty	Bruises
Shock	Burns - 1st or 2nd
Broken Bones	Scrapes/Cuts
Severe Bleeding	Animal Bites
Poisoning	Convulsions/Seizures
Burns - 3rd degree	Earaches
Fever - High	Fever - Low grade
	Nosebleed

90

How to calm a hurt child

- Stay calm.
- Try to explain to the child
  what has happened.

- Tell the child that his parents have
  been called and are on the way home.

- Try to get his mind off of the accident.
  Ask him to sing a song or tell a story.

- Compliment the child.
  Tell him how brave he is.

- Reassure him that you are
  going to stay with him.

91

Guidelines for giving emergency first aid

Your first response duing the beginning
stage of an emergency is critical.
Remember this:

A - Ask for help
I - Intervene
D - Do no further harm

Time is important. The more quickly you
recognize an emergency and the faster
you call for help, the sooner the
child will get help.
Call 911.
Call the parents.

DO NOT DO ANYTHING THAT WILL MAKE THE CHILD'S CONDITION WORSE.

Provide emotional support.

92
Unconscious Child

Call 911 if a child is unconscious,
then call the parents.
There are many causes of unconsciousness and
varying stages of unconsciousness.
Unconsciousness is an abnormal state in which
the victim is not responsive to his surroundings.
An unconscious child may be:
-Drowsy, slipping in and out of consciousness
-Incoherent
-Motionless

· Try to determine what happened.
· Try to wake the child by gently pinching the
bottom of his feet.
· Check to see if he is breathing. Place your ear
near his mouth. Does his chest rise and fall?
· Check ABCs (airway, breathing, circulation).
Call 911 if you cannot identify the
presence of all three.
· Call 911 - STAY ON THE LINE.
· Cover him with a blanket.
· Call the parents.

93
Breathing Difficulty/Choking

If the child is having severe breathing problems, call the parents and 911. It is likely that something is blocking the air passage. Open the mouth and look in. Remove any foreign object if possible.

Difficulty in breathing can be caused by injury, sudden illness, or ongoing medical problems.

Do not place the child in a position he/she finds uncomfortable. Do not place a pillow under the child's head if he/she is lying down.

Do not wait to see if the child is feeling better before calling for help.

Do not give the child anything to eat or drink

If the child is choking on food or some other object, encourage the child to cough until he can breathe freely. If he cannot cough it up, call 911 and ask the operator to coach you through the Heimlich Manuver.

Call the parents.

94
Bleeding (severe)

To control bleeding, apply pressure to seal the edges of the blood vessels while the escaped blood clots to form a self-seal.

Quickly inspect the wound to make sure that nothing is sticking out of it. If there is something sticking out, do not press on it.
Call 911.
Call the parents.

If nothing is sticking out, press firmly on the wound through a gauze pad or a clean towel.

Continue to apply constant pressure until the bleeding stops. If the bleeding does not stop, call 911.

95
Electrical Shock

Children are often fascinated by electrical outlets. Keep them away from electrical outlets!

If a child touches an electrical wire acting as a short circuit, it will burn his fingers. You may only be able to see a tiny bluish mark. Underneath the mark there may be a wide area of damaged tissue. All electrical burns should be treated by a doctor.

If the child is still in touch with the electricity, do not touch him directly.

Shut off the power.

Break the contact between the child and electrical source by using a dry nonconducting object, such as several thicknesses of newspaper.

After you have moved the child away from the current, call 911 and the parents.

Stay with the child. Electricity can cause several internal burns not visible to the naked eye.

96

Poisoning

In a poisoning emergency, rapid first aid is critical. The child may not be able to tell you what has happened. Suspect poisoning if the child suddenly becomes ill for no apparent reason; is found near a toxic substance; has stains on clothing and mouth; or tells you he took or ate medicine or a chemical substance. Signs and symptoms include:

headache
chills, dizziness
fever
nausea, vomiting
blurred vision
unusual breath odor
skin rash
bluish lips
seizures
stupor, unconsciousness

**CALL THE POISON CONTROL
CENTER AND/OR 911.
CALL THE PARENTS**
·Tylenol and asprin can be very toxic.

97

Here is a list of SOME of the potentially poisonous products found in the home:

Window Cleaners
Rubbing Alcohol
Insecticides
Cosmetics
Mothballs
Antifreeze
Paint Remover
Cleaning Fluids
Linseed Oil
Rat Poison
Detergents
Suntan Lotions
Insulation
Fertilizers
Tobacco Products
Aspirin

Acetaminophen (Tylenol)
Perfume
Bleach
Nail Polish Remover
Drain Cleaners
Over Cleaners
Ammonia
Plants
Varnish
Furniture Polish
Medications
Vitamins
Kerosene
Solvents
Disinfectants
Toilet Bowl Cleaners
Floor Polish

* Be aware of the potentially toxic substances in the home.

98
Common Poisonous plants

HOUSE PLANTS

Bird of Paradise
Castor Bean
Dieffenbacchia
English Ivy
Oleander
Philodendron
Poinsettia
Holly

FLOWER GARDEN PLANTS

Daffodil
Hyacinth
Lily of the Valley
Morning Glory
Poppy
Chrysanthemum
Iris
Narcissus
Sweet Pea

99

Consent and Payment

Please refer to Form A in the Appendix.
This form is to be completed and signed
by the parents before they leave their
child in your care.

This form will be used in case you
might have to seek emergency medical
care in their absence.

FORM A
CONSENT & PAYMENT FORM

This form is to be completed and signed by the parents
or legal guardians before they leave the house.

Name of child_____

In the event the child named above is injured or becomes
ill, I understand that the babysitter will attempt to contact
me at the telephone number(s) provided below.

Parent or guardian's name_____

Telephone number(s)_____

In the event that I am not available, I give my permission
to the babysitter to provide first aid for the child named
above and to take appropriate measures, including
contacting emergency medical service and arranging
transportation to _____
or the nearest medical facility.

Parent or guardian's signature_____

Babysitter's signature_____

Medical insurance plan_____

Group number_____ I.D.#_____

* Detach this form and make a copy for each job.

100

Client information and emergency numbers

Please refer to Form B in the Appendix. This form contains important client information and emergency telephone numbers.

This form should be completed before the parents leave their child in your care.

FORM B
CLIENT INFO   Today's Date_____

Client's name_____

Child's name _____

Client's address _____

Babysitter Info

Name_____

Address_____

Telephone number_____

Work schedule _____to_____

Pay rate_____

Important telephone numbers

911
Number(s) where parents can be reached:
_____
_____
Ambulance:_____
Fire Department:_____
Poison control:_____
Pediatrician:_____
Neighbor:_____
Neighbor:_____

* Detach this form and make a copy for each job.

101

Babysitter's Checklist

Please refer to Form C in the Appendix. This form should be filled out jointly by the parents and the babysitter, before the parents leave their child in your care.

FORM C
BABYSITTER'S CHECKLIST
Please help me by answering the following questions:
(Use additional paper if necessary)

1. What time is naptime/ bedtime?

2. What is the bedtime ritual?

3. Does the child need a bath before bedtime?

4. Should the child be fed a snack or meal? If yes, special instructions:

5. What are the child's favorite foods?

6. Are there any foods to avoid?

7. Is the child allergic to anything?

8. Are there any special house rules I should be aware of?

9. How do appliances work? (lights, thermostat, TV, VCR, phone)

10. Can the child go outside?

11. Can the child have friends over?

12. Are there any things the child cannot do?

13. Where will I find: flashlight, first aid kit, towels?

14. What is the child's favorite: toy, book, TV program?

15. Write down precise instructions for giving medicine to the child.

16. Are there any TV programs that are not acceptable to watch?

17. Where will I find diapers and/ or a change of clothes?

18. If the phone rings, should I answer it?

19. Are you expecting any visitors or deliveries?

* Detach this form and make a copy for each job.